Praise for Henry Beissel's *Whe*

I have now read *When Africa Calls* Uhuru through twice. I am able to sense the intensity and indeed the centrality of the message of the poem to modern day reflections on recent world history … It is a special poem to me in the sense that I may have witnessed certain aspects of its inspiring forces. And so I am aware that too this could be a disadvantage to me because I may be looking for the inspiration behind the poem only in physical terms; your presence, for the first time, in the Great Rift Valley with all its natural beauty. I intend to read it again and again because it is not only an explosive, highly creative poetic statement but an invaluable package of rich and varied historical knowledge. I have seen Kenya's wildlife on numerous occasions. But let me admit to you that on no occasion have I seen the animals as vividly as I see them in your poem.

   —**Dr. Francis Imbuga**, novelist/playwright, Kenya

Yesterday I spend most of the day reading and rereading your Africa canto. It is very good indeed, perhaps among your best. You are one of the few poets who capture the mood which is created by our exploded knowledge about the universe and ourselves. It is all so new—a totally different kind of consciousness; a century of knowledge has done little to change old thought-habits; your poetry points in a new direction.

   —**Dr. Wolfgang Bottenberg**, composer

I have just … read your wonderful song to Africa and all of us. Has it been recorded? It should be—I would love to do that. The CBC should be very amenable. No? It is such a deeply emotional and vibrant song it should be heard and reach as wide an audience as possible!

   —**Alan Scarfe**, actor/director

I have now read [the African elegy] several times and it grows, as all good poems should, with each reading. I very much liked your device of your being in Ayorama on a hot and humid summer day and thinking back of your time in Africa; that really works well. I liked too your continued contrasts—the Louis Armstrong/Idi Amin passage in particular...The elegy is a most impressive work and one you must have laboured on long and hard. Congratulations!

   —**Desmond Scott**, actor/director/sculptor

You continue to astonish me … Still going your way and damn the torpedoes. The big opus you're working on (of which *When Africa …* is a part) challenges Whitman. America was enough for him. You're out to net the whole world through all time.

But it's the stance for what's needed now that time and space (and humanity) have become seamless. We have to gobble it all up in order to find our individual place in it. It's a tough task you've set yourself, swinging past pop thought and journalism and on through science to the arts of wonder, wisdom and spirit. But that's us now. The former neatness of expression has been found wanting. Chaotic, uncertain leaps are the new garden tools, are the new imagery of understanding. The poet has to draw from madly disparate sources to stitch together meaning-from-experience-and-insight for the twenty-first century. You're well on your way. Your outrage and kindliness come together as a great force, and inspire us to breathe humane hopes as we leap along to your cadences and vision.

—**Len Peterson**, playwright

… as I have just read *Uhuru* in one sitting the brevity of my note is somehow appropriate as I really am speechless. I have been steeped in first questions, wonderment and pain, and as I struggle for words of appreciation to send you, phrases such as "who knew how to carve//wood into ecstasies …", "Naming the world is like bringing//the lights up on stage. Things appear//to be where and what they are." "A languaged beast//languishes no more." And many other beauties keep coursing through my mind making my project impossible. I know exactly how many years of thinking, studying, observing, meditating and connecting lie behind this wonderful thing you've turned into such "ease". Congratulations.

—**Per Brask**, writer/director

I am impressed on the whole with your African elegy which combines your intellectual engagement with history with a lyrical intensity. You have clearly developed your own style which I can trace back most explicitly to *Cantos North*. The African elegy is like a massive synthesis of your personal wisdom, lyrical instinct, and moral or humane impulse to find earnest truths in the womb of time. Of course, all your various elegies can be read as a massive kaleidoscope of shadows "densing" into a matrix of struggle and liberation. And I always discover something new in your rich diction. Congratulations!

—**Dr. Keith Garebian**, poet, critic/scholar

When Africa Calls Uhuru is a challenging poem and a very moving one, enriched by vocabulary and insights from a wide spectrum of sources and fields of knowledge. Knowing you, Henry, as I do, I try to read it with music in my head, hearing different instruments for the different voices and rhythms. So I see it (or hope to) as a set of symphonic variations on the theme of evil and evolution. It is a cry against cruelty and a plea for love and sharing. And it raises two of the greatest questions of our time—how we come to terms with living in a world defined by chance and what light is to guide man's spirit in place of the religions that have so often betrayed us.

—**Patrick Drysdale**, editor, Oxford, UK

WHEN AFRICA CALLS
UHURU

ESSENTIAL POETS SERIES 302

ONTARIO ARTS COUNCIL
CONSEIL DES ARTS DE L'ONTARIO

an Ontario government agency
un organisme du gouvernement de l'Ontario

Canada Council   Conseil des arts
for the Arts   du Canada

Guernica Editions Inc. acknowledges the support of
the Canada Council for the Arts and the Ontario Arts Council.
The Ontario Arts Council is an agency of the Government of Ontario.

We acknowledge the financial support of the Government of Canada

Henry Beissel

WHEN AFRICA CALLS
UHURU

GUERNICA
EDITIONS

TORONTO • CHICAGO • BUFFALO • LANCASTER (U.K.)
2023

Guernica Founder: Antonio D'Alfonso

Michael Mirolla, editor
Cover and Interior Design: Rafael Chimicatti
Front cover image: *Involutions* (detail), Arlette Francière
Guernica Editions Inc.
287 Templemead Drive, Hamilton (ON), Canada L8W 2W4
2250 Military Road, Tonawanda, N.Y. 14150-6000 U.S.A.
www.guernicaeditions.com

Distributors:
Independent Publishers Group (IPG)
600 North Pulaski Road, Chicago IL 60624
University of Toronto Press Distribution (UTP)
5201 Dufferin Street, Toronto (ON), Canada M3H 5T8

First edition.
Printed in Canada.

Legal Deposit – First Quarter
Library of Congress Catalog Card Number: 2022951816
Library and Archives Canada Cataloguing in Publication
Title: When Africa calls Uhuru / Henry Beissel.
Names: Beissel, Henry, author.
Series: Essential poets; 302.
Description: Series statement: Essential poets series; 302 | A poem.
Identifiers: Canadiana 20220492883 | ISBN 9781771837866 (softcover)
Classification: LCC PS8503.E39 W54 2023 | DDC C811/.54—dc23

Author's Foreword

When Africa Calls Uhuru is the fifth and a pivotal section in my epic cycle, *Seasons of Blood. Uhuru* is Swahili for 'freedom', and the struggle for freedom is the central dynamic in this entire opus.

In the process of writing the epic, it became a global search for what it means to be human. It was therefore inevitable that the search would take me to Africa, specifically to the Rift Valley in Kenya, where our ancestors finally came down from the trees about two million years ago to live as *Homo erectus* on the ground.

We are animals: hominids, cousins of chimpanzees and bonobos with whom we share 98.8% of our DNA. Why, then, are we so different from them? The fundamental difference, I decided, was the development of language skills that enabled us to name all objective reality, all matter, organic and mineral, as well as their actions and interactions, thereby bringing all to analytical consciousness and thus learning to understand and to manipulate them creatively.

While chimps have little choice but to live by the whims of nature, by its chance actions upon them, we humans have a large measure of control over these forces and can direct them to serve our own purposes, preferences and designs. We call that process civilization, and after ten thousand years of civilization we should be living in a world as paradisiacal as the laws of living and dying would allow.

It was not until well into the writing of *Seasons of Blood* that I realized what was driving me: a desperate effort to understand the monstrous contradictions between the world such as a creature that calls itself 'Homo sapiens', the 'wise human', would want to create—a world of love, peace, beauty and happiness—and the brutal reality of the human world, especially today.

No animal comes anywhere near our understanding of the world, and yet no animal practices murdering its own kind and destroying the environment on which it depends for its survival. Humans do. How did we get ourselves into the mess of perpetual wars and catastrophic climate change? How do we reconcile Beethoven's "Ode to Joy" with nuclear missiles, Horton Holiday Village with Auschwitz Concentration Camp, and Mahatma Gandhi with Vlad the Impaler?

A crucial step in the pursuit of my objective was the decision to include Africa in the global journey of my poem because the human struggle for freedom happened there first and on two levels: the deliverance of at least one species of living being, us, from the chains of the non-conscious servitude of mute creatures and the liberation of civilized human beings from the chains, the cruelties and the slavery of colonialism. The first had taken its most dramatic step in the Rift Valley in Kenya and to feel what it may have been like I flew to Nairobi. The second struggle against the evils of colonialism was still going on all across Africa and elsewhere: what were its roots?

I spent a few weeks crisscrossing the Rift Valley, specifically the Maasai Mara grassland, rejoicing in the company of wild elephants, lions, leopards, hippos, wildebeest, cheetahs and gazelles, to mention just some of the abundant wildlife that extends into the neighbouring Serengeti Park in Tanzania. I threw myself with gusto into the fauna and flora because I wanted to feel what it was like for our ancestors to climb down from the safety of their arboreal world and accept the survival challenge from creatures faster, more powerful and more brutal than themselves. Given the superior forces they faced, it's a miracle that they prevailed and embarked on the magnificent and triumphant journey on foot that eventually led to the conquest of the whole planet. How come we had lost our way in the process? My imagination and my emotions were on fire.

My good fortune was that I had the guidance and support of a Kenyan writer. When planning my trip, I had gone to the Kenyan High Commissioner in Ottawa and asked him if he could recommend a writer who might be willing to assist me with my research in Africa, a continent wholly unknown to me. I met with an enthusiastic response and upon my arrival, the distinguished Kenyan playwright and novelist Francis Imbuga, till then a total stranger to me, was waiting for me at the airport in Nairobi.

During the weeks I spent researching, Francis proved to be an invaluable guide. The passion for his homeland and his profound understanding of it sent me to the right places everywhere from Mombasa on the Indian Ocean to Wenyange Village in the West where he was born and where he introduced me to his family and friends. Francis was a caring and insightful person, and we soon became bosom friends. Alas, Francis died in 2016, and I want to dedicate *When Africa Calls* Uhuru to him as my memorial to express my profound gratitude for his friendship and for opening the heart and mind of Kenya to me.

When I returned home, my imagination and my emotions were alive with what I had experienced and learnt in Kenya. To find the right words for the complexity of what I had been forced to confront was a bit like what my African ancestors faced when they abandoned the safe canopy of their jungle for the challenges on the common ground. In the end, the structure of the poem emerged naturally as a drama with four characters when I filtered my experiences through four optics: those of nature, science, history and the imagination. The different voices are identifiable both by their diction and their place on the page.

Francis Imbuga's reaction to the completed poem was generously enthusiastic. He claimed he had never seen Africa through such lucid eyes. "This poem should've been written by an African," he enthused. I replied: "It was. I'm just a few generations removed from my African ancestors." I hope the reader can hear the different voices, always remembering my maxim: *Words point / to what cannot be said.* In poetry, music and imagery are often more articulate.

Henry Beissel
(March 20, 2022)

Africa,
Idle giant
Basking in the sun,
Sleeping, snoring,
Twitching in dreams:
Diseased with chronic illness,
Choking with black ignorance,
Chained to the rock of poverty,
And yet laughing,
Always laughing and dancing,
The chains on his legs
Jangling,
Displaying his white teeth
In bright pink gum,
Loose white teeth
That cannot bite,
Joking, giggling, dancing …

Okot p'Bitek, *Song of Ocol*

Nothing dissolves the mind's fogs as limpidly
as a summer morning mist forcing the outward eye
to look inward. Far away I see a black sun rise
that scorches deserts and steams up jungles
on a continent closer to my heart than all
the tall tales of religion. Once upon many
beginnings I was born there—so was this song,
and you, my uncertain reader. Once upon a crack
of ice or fire we put our feet on the ground
and walked, heads held high, the whole length
of Africa into this labyrinth of words echoing
uhuru from the Arab deserts in the north
all the way south to the cape of Zululand.

Uhuru uhuru uhuru—
is that the grey voice of an owl
lost in the clouds that have come
down to earth this morning?
Dark call muffled in the damp
gauze stuffed between ash maple
pine and spruce that packs
fields farms and fences,
till nothing remains but vapour
and the world returns to some
primordial state—no shapes
no colour nothing but shades
of grey even the sun is no more
than a creamy smear
like some ointment
to heal an injury of nature.

Out of the mist that hides summer
from this dawn come voices
once more voices worn thin
travelling by chance between ice ages
impact craters and continents adrift
a Babel of voices spinning unrecorded
histories from memories as webbed
as spiders' nets, with meshes
wide enough for whole generations
to pass through, yet looped to catch
what keeps the mind alive—voices
their tongues lost to dust before
they could tell the tale of a tribe
that learnt to name a summer in the mist.

I hear the winds of history throb
in the jibs and mizzens, mainsails
and lateens of argosies, caravels,
dhows and galleons hugging a fickle
coast from cape to cape struggling
against a hostile sea I hear the plash
of oars the soft crunch of keels
in the sands of Abidjan DeKaap
and Zanzibar I hear commands
curses shouts and prayers in Arabic
Portuguese Dutch English French
as men come ashore to discover
a dark continent they never knew
deep down at their own hearts' core:
a black paradise where the adders
and vipers of their worst nightmares
had made their nests aeons ago.

The sun is devouring the morning
mist now and a familiar summer world
fades into focus image by image
like a photographic print in its developer
nameless silhouettes densing into leaves
branches—a tree! greening as grass ferns
shrubs vines flowers precipitate still nameless
from grey wisps like a green rubbing on tracing
paper a full spectrum of greens concocted
in the chlorophyll mills of every plant
an Ontario flora surfacing in waves
between 495 and 515 nm that make July here
greener than a sea of emeralds. Then a footpath
the toolshed a fencepost loom—intimations
of a different kind: you and I emerge from dawn.

The white men who melted from the mists
of the sea never knew the black men
who peeled from the shadows of trees
were the brothers and sisters they left
thousands of generations earlier in search
of fresh fields and adventures. Blinded
by divine delusions and the black gold
of slavery they saw only savages
born to serve their needs and appetites.
Jungles deserts even the rivers
with their errant courses resisted them
but treaty by treaty and treachery
by treachery they spread like a slow
terminal disease and cankered Africa
when they thought they conquered it.

Something called *uhuru* across the continent
till the rains picked it up in their seasons
and beat it into the trees and the forests
drummed *uhuru* up and down the great rift
valley between smoking craters and implacable
escarpments where humongous herds of wild
beasts thundered across grassland and rivers
long before *uhuru* meant freedom long before
language found meaning in a meaningless world
and there was speech to utter or sense to heed it—

Suddenly a flock of starlings
sensing perhaps an early fall
scatter a last fog patch
in the trees with their high
pitched alarums like the chatter
of agitated monkeys I hear
out of the green and steamy heat
hissing growling grunting
and howling, croaking squealing
and baying, snarling roaring
belching bellowing and braying
voices everywhere the voices
of feeding mating and dying
fill every crack and crevice
in the silences of Africa's
teeming forests and savannahs:
a cacophony of life cresting
in the skull with a big bang.

Could all that have been
prefigured all the myriad
forms of life struggling
to adapt to the never
ending upheavals of oceans
and continents and that last
blood-stained chapter
from stone to stromatolite
to stock-market—could all
that have been contained
in the unimaginable
fraction of an attosecond
before the atom before
the quark even before Planck
time at the tredecillionth part (10^{-43})
of a second of there being
anything at all and not
rather nothing when the four
forces that hold everything
everywhere in place now
were one and indivisible
in a space tinier than
a single proton that
contained everything
we know and can ever
come to know? How
do you get from nothing
to the stars and trees
and from there to misery?
In that singular atto-moment
of perfection outside space
where was the flaw
that put pen to paper
to ask the question why
put pain to pleasure

in that singular and ultimate
black hole where everything
was nothing why four
forces one and
indivisible
fractured time
into galaxies
why the sun why
Africa why the
question any
question
why you
why
I?

In the large picture window of my study the sun
now paints a summer landscape in silent motion:
clouds the mist raised trek eastward across a blue
savannah like a never-ending drive of shaggy
primordial mammoths in search of grass and water
shooed by the wide gestures of ash and tamarack
whose branches wave them on solemnly as in some
slow motion wind the tall tern spruce nods gravely
at the mystery it mediates between heaven and earth.
From the green scramble on the ground foul smelling
cow parsnip thrusts umbels at the light, the barbed
devil's club whose septic spines have pierced many
a moccasin and legging is ripening red berries
clustered like drops of fresh blood over large green
leaves. Treehopper nymphs tumble from elm twigs
to moult in the clovered grass into bugs that mimic
black thorns or green excrescences birds overlook.
A bluejay swoops down, its shadow screaming—

screaming at whom? Rosita's
eyes stare at me unforgotten
and unforgetting from the jungle
foliage looped in my skull.
Her spring has come and gone
but I see her pain still
in the eyes of children
everywhere. Though all
the saxophones in Dixieland
lament, the world goes on
spinning its idiot tales
of blood and tears over
and over: today it's Kigali,
yesterday it was Mogadishu
and Sarajevo, the day before:
Soweto Beirut El Salvador
East Timor the West Bank
Northern Ireland South Vietnam
on and on tomorrow and tomorrow …
In what Africa of the heart
was violence born? I've watched
the big cats in the wilds
of Kenya and found them fierce
in defence and feeding, but tender
with their own and tolerant
of others. What happened
on the way to wisdom?
Where? When? Why?

Comets and asteroids struck time and again
shaking our planet to its molten core shaping
a *terra infirma* in cataclysms of oceans and continents
extremities of climate and atmosphere the violence
of earthquakes floods cyclones volcanic convulsions

Permian Norian Cretaceous in countless nameless
catastrophes over and over yesterday's victor
vanquished today till land and sea were left dead
for millennia as trilobites lycaenops and dinosaurs
along with countless species too bizarre for words
vanished forever in evolution's teeming blind
alleys where a shift of air or water current
can make the fittest unfit for the new world.

Beginnings? Where
did *homo sapiens*
begin? Begin what?
To breathe? When we
crawled from the sea.
Why? To eat and be
eaten. Why? To live?
Why live? To talk?
To think? Yes think
why think why
when all I must do
is eat and make
love?—Love? Why
when did it begin?
In the stromatolite
four thousand million
years ago where one
celled bacteria learnt
to use light to make
sugar? Those same
immortal chloroplasts
toil still in every plant
to feed all living creatures.
Or did the human
tragicomedy begin

when the triassic curtain
rose and a reptilian
mouse appeared on stage
to manufacture milk
from sweat and learn
to climb trees and thus
survived two hundred
million years of predators
and cosmic violence
to become the first
primate? … Beginnings?

July 1, 1858: Darwin
and Wallace published
papers that abolished
beginnings. There are
only junctures and
something is gained
in every change of
direction something
is inevitably lost.
A twitch in grey slime,
a gyral quirk or a twist
of vertebrae or chords
in the throat precipitated
the neocortex that posits
probabilities fifteen
billion years earlier
to create a universe
ex nihilo fit
by a law too simple
for human understanding.
What has no beginning
for us must begin too.

Once upon a thousand times ice crusts co-opted
rains to creep miles thick south and north
from the poles, compacting rock, reshaping
landscapes beyond recognition and forcing life
to redesign scales as pelt and fur, and to retreat
into the shrinking territories of the sun.
In the unforgiving drama of dying and adapting
a hairy simian had gained a firm grasp
on branches reprogramming feet to move hand
over hand and relocating eyes to get perspective
on a green world and turn flat images
into solid objects that remained nameless yet
for another fifty million years. Now that drought
thinned forests squeezed in the tropic vise
deserted him australopithecus thumbed his nose
at ice ages and vanishing habitats and walked
straight into savannahs beyond all horizons
to test among sabre-tooth cats and elephants
the tools that make us killers and creators.

They came from Europe to all
the coasts of Africa in the garb
of culture, treating natives
like savages for they were savages
themselves—despite the chamberpots
replete with whiskey and wisdom
they came to empty in Africa and
refill with the continent's riches.
What they called trade was plunder
for they bartered at the point
of their guns, practising the art
of humiliation on a people who had
mastered the arts of bronze
and ivory, who knew how to carve

wood into ecstasies, how to cast
iron into tool and weapon, and
to fire terracotta long before
a Palestinian carpenter preached
universal brotherhood to those
who came to deny it, laying waste
the black man's courts and kingdoms,
ripping apart the fabric clans
and tribes had woven over the millennia
to contain pride and anger, scorning
their songs and dances that nurtured
the bonds of fellowship and affection
greed corrodes quick as an acid
iron. An unholy trinity of merchants
missionaries and military sat
at sundown, and mocked Africa,
casting lots as black men rounded up
their brothers and sisters
and sold them to be slaves.

In the harbour of Dakar
on Gorée Island stands
a slave house, its walls
saturated with the cries
of a hundred million
men women and children
whose only crime was
the colour of their skin.
Herded into pens they were
measured and examined
—the men's muscles
the women's breasts
the children's teeth—
and those found wanting

or sick were tossed out
the door right into
the sea as fodder
for sharks. The others
waited in darkness:
ankle irons spiked
through the foot and
itenu rings driven
through the lips
to quell the rebellious
they were fattened
to 140 lbs to fetch
the best price for
a voyage in the dark
holds of pestilent ships
where one third of them
perished, the rest
auctioned off across
the ocean to be
whipped and worked
chained and lynched
at white folks' pleasure
or displeasure.

Africa, you still bear
the stigma of our shame
though those who left
as slaves are free now
because they did not
shut their mouths
and they would not
forget their songs
forget their dances:

Blow man blow
that horn man
blow the blues
tongue that reed
slide the pitch
smooth as skin
the cymbals whisper
shake it baby
let the drums shake
an' swing the flesh
ain't no one there
to take care
of you an' me—
jus' you an' me

paw that bass man
till the blood sings
blue the blues bro
let the trumpet yell
at sun an' moon
life's a grief an' a thrill
baby move baby
wind down the day
pluck the strings
like they's nipples
ain't no one there
to take care
of you an' me—
jus' you an' me

jazz up your lovin'
the night is hot an' sweet
we ain't goin' nowheres
jus' dancin' to the beat
life's a kick an' a jump
lonely as the stars

in your eyes
baby oh baby
move it shake it
while I blow
my heart out
ain't no one there
to take care
of you an' me—
jus' you an' me.

In the hush that follows I hear
the cries and groans of tortured
flesh. The drummer yes, the singer
the philosopher yes, but is it cool
to listen to a drunkard slaughter
his own kind, to a big mouth
commanding executions, a noisy
half-wit who dismembers his own wife,
or a savage who enjoys flogging
thieves to death with rifle butts?
Their victims' cries darken Africa's
skies: no other animal on earth exacts
such punishment from its own. Every
continent is awash with premeditated
self-inflicted human pain and misery.
Are homicidal maniacs the measure
of a species that struggled for five
million years up the brain's convoluted
paths to reach the light at the end
of the tunnel of its five senses?
Must consciousness either remain
dormant in the mists of unknowing
or wake up and walk Okot p'Bitek
hand in hand with Jean-Bédel Bokassa,

Louis Armstrong with Idi Amin,
Martin Luther King hand in hand
with Joseph Désiré Mobutu, and
the madman of Moroni with Nelson
Mandela—marching in syncopated time
uhuru beyond good and evil
where the way up is as the way down?

                    Eyes take the measure of far flung valleys
              where Africa is tearing itself apart inch by inch
                and peer through a blue haze fed by volcanoes
                  the exhalations of life and the dust hoof herds
                     and wind-hoses raise—glistening black
              white-edged eyes survey an obscure map of colours
                   shapes shades and movement for signs of food
                  and danger. The stars stirred no great longing
                   in the night though a tiny skew in the spine had
                    already launched their descendants on a flight
              to the moon. Aeons passed speechless as mountains
                    rose and sea levels fell. Speciation flourished
                    while forests died giving a chance to the crafty
              young grasses which had harnessed the wind to spread
                 a treeless savannah across whole continents—a vast
              green carpet to welcome all the world's cats and cattle.
              And they came: lion and leopard, aurochs and horse,
                    forcing *homo habilis* to spend a couple of million
              years reengineering his hindlegs and perfecting the art
                  of walking before his elevation to the rank of *erectus*.

The sun is soaring toward noon.
Outside my study tufted vetch
coils tendrils through the grass.
Alfalfa butterflies tumble back

and forth between flowers up
and down like lemon petals
in an eccentric wind. Yet
the air is so still the buzz
of insects is loud enough
to mimic a distant plane.

I dream of Africa where fossils
speak louder than the follies
of superman. From the remote
aegyptopithecus whose passion
for fruit high in the trees
made them four-handed
to *homo sapiens sapiens*
whose larger brain has
yet to accommodate wisdom—
a handful of teeth must tell
the tale of a million generations
and trace the thin red lines
through the trials and errors
of primates as species and sub-species
come and go through the rapidly
revolving doors of evolution.
Wit and will like speed and strength
are at the mercy of pure chance.
If the Cretaceous comet had missed
this planet by a megameter
a sauronithoide might now
be writing this poem for a different
indifferent age of dinosaurs.
Or if the comet impacting Jupiter
today had crashed into earth
instead human history would end
tomorrow in a cloud of dust.

Would dinosaurs have made history
an idiot's tale like ours?
In the territories of the mind
nothing stands between the cannibal
Bokassa and Botticelli's Venus
but the sea and a different perspective.

Seeing is remembering. Because I was there
alongside you in a camp by the river winding
through the savannah, a small band we were,
moving with the seasons, our diet changed
from fruit-eating solipsism in the trees
to roots dug up and meat scavenged
that called for shared meals—we shared
everything: food, caves, children,
we shared the shade in the midday heat
and our bodies' warmth and needs at night,
we shared the stones to pound tubers
and crush bones to extract the marrow,
we slept on shared matted steads,
we shared grooming, gathering, guarding
and play—if we'd not shared you and I
would not be here to tell the story,
I know, I saw it with my own eyes
by the Mara river, saw what they saw:

a herd of hippos cooling humongously
in the muddy waters, their bulging eyes
protruding from time to time like periscopes
as they snort for air, flicking their tiny
ears; on the embankment, immobile as logs,
crocodiles, pinned down by the vicious light;
behind them a troop of baboons, young

and old, scampering through thorn bushes,
noisy as a nursery, paying no attention
to the lion in the shade of a candelabrum tree
courting his lioness as tenderly as any lover
in heat, and when she is aroused they mate;
just then three wart hogs appear, tusks
curled like handlebar moustaches, they hurry
single file across the clearing, stop
curtly in their tracks, take in the scene
and hurry on as though late for an appointment.

Where is the aggressor? Where aggression?
Not even the herd of elephants trumpeting
along the river can trouble the shared
territory: no imperatives to kill
except when hunger strikes or the young
must be defended. Sharing calls for
sounds and gestures of assent, not
for expenditures in violence and venom.

Beware of army uniforms
beribboned and bedecked
with medals like a buffoon's
costume: they are the primp
of butchers—like Idi the syphilitic
who slaughtered three hundred
thousand of his own people
kept the choicest parts
of his choicest foes
in the fridge to eat
with an imbecile's bloodshot
eyes and slobbering grin
he crushed the pearl of Africa

under his blood-spattered boots
till only dust was left
ashes grief and pain.

Cry, my beloved Africa,
cry for your women
because the hyena
of Uganda is not alone
in his madness: too many
men's manhood is nothing
but spears and swagger.
Your women carry
your burdens
on their heads
and shoulders
erect as bamboo
they walk trails
and paths through
desert and jungle
mountains and savannah
they balance earthen
water jugs and fruit
from the fields where
they seed and weed
to wrest a harvest
from stone and heat
while their man
struts his cock
in the village
brandishing
his rhetoric
to prove
if all fails
at the point

of a machete
that he is
who he is not:
Simba the Lion!
and that he is not
who he is meant to be:
the man it took
threeandahalf
billion years
to wrest from the
intractable
elements
to come through
consciousness
to love.

Ask the women
whom age bends low
because they carried
too many bunches
of bananas too many
loads of bamboo and ebony
cane and cassava,
each of them
the fittest
vessel to carry
the seeds of love safely
through disease
and disaster across
a million millennia
beyond mutation and death—
ask them about pride.
Close to the ground
they move still

like slow freighters
heavy with the past's
consignment to the future
challenging you to join
hands in the dance of life:

Harambee!
the once saintly
Kenyatta called,
Let's all join together!
Paint your bodies,
paint your faces,
tie *lacucuku* rattles to your legs!
Beat the drums and
make a circle,
dance for rain, for seeds and harvest!
Shake and shuffle,
churn your belly,
dance for love, for death and weddings!
Stomp the earth and
sing to heaven,
dance for joy, for birth and sorrow—
harambee!

Laugh at the priest
fondling your full breasts
with his arid eyes
denying his lust and your dance.
Mock the soldier
with his gun
ready for the dance of war:
tell him to come
with a hoe to plant a garden.
Scorn the merchant

with his money
dancing on the bottom line:
teach him that the price
of life is love.
Shake your hips
and roll your belly
dance oh dance for friends and lovers
for today is
yesterday's tomorrow
a mango tree
ripe for picking
when you dance and sing together
make a circle
for the spirits
joy and love
will dance forever
in your hot and perishable flesh.
Harambee!

Croon man croon
dark and husky
as the jungle
blood dances
hot as head
baby hold me
feel me tight
the bass baby
the beat feel
baby the drums
call Africa
cool man cool
the music swings
the piano shake

you heart crazy
shake she thigh
and throw he leg
blow man blow
that clarinet
high higher high
baby blow me
all the way
to Africa blow
me in the sky!

Today I'm back where my cradle stood:
it's as hot and humid, still and heavy here
as in the heart of any tropical rain forest.
A blue haze hangs in the listless trees
and even the sharp sumac looks limp.
The air is panting in a sweat, birds
are dozing under their feathers, frogs
gasp silently by the pond, the mosquitoes
have taken shelter in the cedars or
cling to the dank shadows under blades
of wilting grass. The day has developed
a breath smelling sweet and sour
of stagnant pools seminal ooze
and saprogenic slime. The deer-flies
are frenzied by the heat and attack
kamikaze style on delta wings, cicadas
wake up to shrill the torpor, and
the raspberries' red and pearly drupelets
look rich and lusty in the sweltering
light that suppurates from a glaucous sky
where the sun is fiercely coming to a head.

Our ancestors endured here
heat waves worse than this—
temperatures hot enough
to fry the brain, insects
larger and more lethal
than a poisoned arrowhead,
predators as callous
as the stone they fashioned
into tools, and parasitic
worms eating them alive
in stages of such pain
to put any inquisitor to shame:

          the invisible armies
          of amoebae bacilli
          cocci spirilla and
          viruses commanded by
          the tyrannical sun
          conquer the mightiest
          conqueror; they give you
          no choice: lockjaw
          bilharzia leprosy
          and hepatitis—dysentery
          alone kills ten million
          children under five
          each year in Africa
          where the ubiquitous
          mosquito bites at random
          spreading malaria
          and yellow fever,
          the tsetse fly
          frantically injects
          the sleeping sickness
          whose coma is terminal,

the tiny buffalo gnat
lays its eggs
in any open wound
where they hatch
and ulcerate the skin
till river blindness
breaks out and kills you
unless the excruciating
itch from head to toe
drives you to kill
yourself first;
the filovirus will
blister your skin
rip your flesh
in shreds till you
vomit and cough up
your throat, your tongue
and your trachea
in bits and pieces
with black blood
and you succumb
to seizures
while parasitic worms
burrow through
their victims' insides
till they bleed
from mouth and rectum
with the green monkey
disease or hemorrhage
to death internally
with snail's fever
which still infects
200 million people
annually throughout
the disadvantaged world

—so many painful ways
to die, so few to survive!

Yet we date our succession
back billions of generations
directly to the primal ooze,
each one of us travelled
that desperate ecstatic path
to consciousness and even
our first bacterial ancestors
learnt that those who share
fare better in the battle
to survive. There never was
a paradise at the beginning:
it is an island dreams created
in a treacherous capricious sea.
There is only the horror and
the happiness of knowing being.

The ocean that gave birth to life
was not Homer's wine dark sea
or Botticelli's benign water,
nor even Shakespeare's wind-obeying
or Delacroix's tempestuous deep—
more soup than sea it was leached
from molten rock mineral and ore
in a million years of rain between
volcanoes spewing perpetual magma
and asteroids the size of continents
comets meteors pummelling the planet
till all the elements danced
up a storm of atoms breaking
molecules down reuniting particles
by electrical charges and discharges

in a furious slop crater by crater
where amino acids time and again
joined forces only to be wrenched
apart again and rejoined
till a short single-strand RNA
catalyzed protein and by a random
felicitous mistake replicated
as DNA ... and life began—
by the grace of amphiphiles,
hydrothermal vents, fool's gold,
or a gift from other stars?
Beginnings? Minerals know how to
replicate a pattern but they cannot
multiply. The first membrane formed
somewhere between amino acids
and nucleotides became the binding
for the book of life the DNA began
to write in a four-letter alphabet
etching a code in carbon blocks
that describes and determines all
that lives all that lived and all
that will ever come to live
by mitosis or meiosis chromosome
crossover inversion or point
mutation in the genetic spiral
whose elegant symmetry belies the crude
and blundering deviance of evolution.

The stone is but a step
from the flower and the worm
but a remove from the root
of trees. What separates
the mammal from the microbe
is only a matter of time.

We are the issue of exploding
stars that seeded a galactic
cloud and precipitated earth,
progeny of the rocks, cousins
to every plant and animal
under the sun. What their host
calls a disease is a feast
for parasites and death
is a hotbed for bacteria
and scavengers. Our world
has no seams: greening breathing
dancing and growing, feeding
mating dying and flowing
are the hop and the scotch
of nature's hazardous game
connecting all and everything
so long as the rules are not broken.

Who has the power makes
and breaks the rules
till the power breaks
him: Cpt. Jean-Bédel
needed a special
uniform for all the
medals he gave himself
till on a sizzling day
he made himself
Sa Majesté impériale
l'Empereur Bokassa Ier
in Bokassa Stadium on
Bokassa Avenue in
a coronation robe studded
with two million pearls
placing a $ 2 million crown
with a 138 carat diamond

on his head in a country
in central Africa with
an annual per capita
income of $ 250 and
250 km of paved highway
connecting the 250 imperial
statues and palaces—
his friend Valéry Giscard
footed the bills in the name
of another delusion of
power which stipulates that
a colony must remain
a colony forever if under
a different name a different
ruler the rules remain
the same: the poor grow
poorer because the rich
grow richer so long as
someone else pays
and Giscard (in return
for gifts of diamonds) paid
out of his people's pockets
for Jean-Bédel's madness
mayhem and murder
till the Imperial cannibal
clubbed 80 children
to death for refusing to wear
the new national school
uniform adorned with his
Imperial mug and medals.
'He's not that bad,'
the wife of an American
missionary told reporters
with Christian charity,
'there's complete religious

freedom here? After all,
Sa Majesté impériale converted
twice back and forth between
god's learned son and
his illiterate prophet,
depending on who paid
how much, and he atoned
for his slaughter
by fathering 30 children
on 9 wives—admittedly
a far cry from the Master
of the Spear who claimed
to have begotten 500 progeny
on 100 wives—still,
the bottom line leaves
only a net loss of
50 children slain,
which is *not that bad.*

Cry for your children,
my beloved Africa,
where my cradle stood,
for they are still
being murdered
or they die from hunger,
disease and heartbreak,
die before they can walk,
die before they can talk,
because their fathers
will not deny the rich
are growing richer
perfecting the cruelties
their colonial masters
invented, but bossman

is bossman black or white
the poor are growing poorer
hair curly or straight
and Africa is free now
to be its own master
and must master itself
to dance for its 500 gods.

Beware
of the tidings
of missionaries:
they say *mercy*
when they mean
mercenary
and *save*
when they mean
slave!
They bring you
to your knees
with your eyes shut
they rob you blind
taking your land
in exchange for some
holy Humpty Dumpty
from the nursery
of Neanderthal man.

The negro is a child,
said the once saintly
man from Lambaréné,
*and children must be
chastised.* Then he played
Bach on his organ
and attended to their pain.

Cry for your men, Africa,
because they deny their children
their humanity, deny them the dignity
of schools where they could learn
to turn words into wings to rise above
the slimy exchanges of money
and copulation, to fly to a cape
of good hope where they can be
free and equal under the black-hot sun.
Your men dream Mercedes Benz
instead of freedom though all
the valleys and their mountains
lakes and rivers from sea to sea
the plains and forests cry *uhuru* …

which means freedom is the path life has chosen
from prokaryotes to protozoa elaborating cilia
and flagella in the prison of their cells evolving
ever changing associations for three thousand
million years to constitute the first fish captive
of the sea struggling to turn fins into crutches
turning fins into legs for amphibians turning
swim bladders into lungs to live in the air
and run as reptiles the whole length of the land
to mammals climbing trees learning to walk
upright as hominids to propel themselves
beyond the wildest dream of any bird to soar
into space and escape the hold the earth has
over us and fly free *per aspera ad astra*.

The path the primate took had many junctions
and more pitfalls than a terminal moraine.
From dryopithecus to this day we clambered

through a landscape in permanent revolt.
Gondwanaland is still exploding in slow motion
raising range upon range of heaven storming
mountains from the Alps to the Himalayas.
Heat waves are short interglacial recesses
when glaciers melting and with torrential rains
drill rivers through rock—Rhine, Danube,
Ganges, Volga, Mackenzie, and in Africa
they carved the sweeping course of Congo
and Zambezi, Nile and Niger, and cascaded
the waters of the Limpopo, Ogowe and
Volta fuming into the sea. But the ice
always returned, spreading from the poles,
sucking up the oceans to bury most of the land
under a lid of ice a mile thick until
the Mediterranean dried up and the estuaries
of the Nile and the Rhône became waterfalls
a mile down into the salt-crusted basin.

The ebb and flow of weathers and tectonics
left Africa in the shape of a heart
and placed it at the centre of the globe
midway between Asia and America, Arctic
and Antarctica, at the centre of life. Here
an ape met the challenge of an alien
environment and blood began to beat
in temples booming hot like a dark drum
calling all the world to consciousness.
Generations of primates came and went
driven by cold and curiosity scavenging
then hunting their way across the planet
fighting mock battles to maintain order
and returning taller bolder more skilful
always on the move tools chipped and flaked

always changing—the teeth the jaw the brow
more graceful, nomads following the migrations
of rivers and cattle grass and sunshine
turning grunts and squeals into bonds
of affection refining the clan and the vocal
chords growing more determined the hand
the walk the chin the skull more domed
till the brain had tripled and—there!

        they stood—the first *homo sapiens* couple
        coming to know their image in the still pool
        as their own knowing growing to love
        what they knew that they must be
        wanderers on a journey free to choose
        a destination in search of no matter
        where or why the true measure of the mind
        is a question mark. Perhaps they were
        moved to tears by what they felt they saw
        they knew in that shared unrecorded moment
        when millions of neurons fired and burnt
        an immemorial film from their eyes—
        in that first blaze they must have marvelled
        mute at the splendour and the mystery
        of the land- and lifescape stretched out
        below the mind's peak and they saw
        in a drenching rain the tears in all
        things as they listened to the dark
        thunder mourn a loss of innocence
        for which there are still no words.

Naming the world is like bringing
the lights up on stage. Things appear
to be where and what they are.

Each word recreates the world
giving it colour shape motion
place... and soon tropical birds
performed their ritual for the just
awakening mind in a paradise
of the imagination: the black and white
boubou with their bell-whistle-and-croak
routine deep in dark thickets;
the choral toogel-de-doogle
of the speckled red and yellow
barbet breeding among termites;
the shrill kingfisher diving
for small-fry on malachite wings;
the hornbill with casqued and curved
beak grunting like a lion as it
walls in its mate in a mud-and-dung
cell to breed; the lilac-breasted
roller in feathered finery
of a splendour fit for a wedding;
the long-legged secretary bird
stalking the savannah in silence;
crested with a headdress
worthy of a Bantu chieftain,
or any of the thousand birds
of Africa—the golden weavers
gregarious in their globed nests,
the parasitic whydahs, the multi-coloured
sunbirds glittering in flowering
trees, the spectacular bush
shrikes and parrots, bishops
cutthroats lovebirds and bee-eaters
waxwings turacos woodpeckers
white-eyes and pittas, the parasitic
flycatchers with their long cinnamon
tails and the red-faced apalises

singing in the desert scrub—
a chirping warbling cheeping
twittering piping trilling
squawking hooting and whistling
musical riot that left the first
man and woman speechless—

but they soon found words, words and
more words for to name is to share
and they came to know what the birds
in the air knew already and all the beasts
in the water and on land—that to share
is to survive and sharing they tested
and honed words and more words
for to name precisely is to understand
and they came to know what the birds
in the air and all the beasts in the water
and on land never knew—
that to understand is to be human.

Thus *homo sapiens sapiens* was born in the great rift
valley when once again the advancing ice encircled
Africa and Tuba exploded with the force of a hundred
Krakatoas and blew 2,000 km³ out of the earth into the sky
to beget a global winter of many years that only the fittest
survived. Where a geological day earlier, hippos browsed
in the blazing sun by the Thames, polar bears were now
hunting seals while to the south a most adaptable primate
rewired its brain and grew Broca's bump on its cranium
to accommodate speech and comprehension. Soon this
curious creature sharpened its tongue along with its tools
and outgrew the scavenging competition of vultures
and hyenas. As summer returned small bands followed
the receding ice, the men hunting wild oxen, red deer

and horses, elephants and rhinos, the women gathering
nuts fruit roots, the children laughing and learning—
they spread across every continent to begin their journey
to the stars, building spaceships out of words determined
to leave the birds to their trees and inhabit the skies.

A languaged beast
languishes no more.
Words are oil
in curiosity's flames,
salt in the wounds
of ignorance and folly,
water on the mills
of invention—words
are the arsenic of anger
and the spice of love,
a poet's dream and
a politician's nightmare,
for they name to tell
the truth; they make
all things appear
to be what they are:
debatable—
and in the heat
of argument they are
lost unless you raise
your voice to song.

I have travelled the seven seas
and every continent to sing to you
of my voyage that started before
it began and that will go on after
it ends. The whirlwinds of change

blow forever on these smooth coasts
pushing Africa across the equator.
I sing of the adventure of being
human. You and I are never
the same twice. Even as I sing
and you listen we move beyond
the words that express us.
We too have reached the equator
of our destiny. Our tools
and weapons have outstripped and
outmanoeuvered us on a power trip
that leaves our fellow-travellers
gasping. Even our knowledge
has left us to the mercies
of machines. I want to sing
but the cacophonies of hatred
are louder and I must bear
witness today for tomorrow
will soon be our yesterday.

Once upon a time war was a ritual,
the loser yielding place and mate
but not his life, a ritual enacted
by birds and beetles, whales, lions
and chimpanzees. Should not
the primate with the double wisdom
have been as smart? Instead
Shaka with the tiny penis forged
assegai into swords and slaughtered
his astonished foes. Forcing young
and old, men and women, to bear arms
he marched killing and conquering

the Umfolozi River to forge
a Zulu kingdom for his mother
Nandi, the Female Elephant. Bloody
was his revenge for his diminished manhood:
witch doctors with dry gourds
in their hair smelled out his enemies
and with the black tails of wildebeest
condemned them to the fire-hardened
needle-pointed bamboo hammered home
with painstaking accuracy and slowness.

Apart from us, is there or has there
ever been among the vigintillions
of animals and species on this planet
past and present a single one capable
of forcing a needled-pointed stake
through the rectum up the spine
of a fellow-creature and enjoy watching
it writhe to death like a worm on a hook,
but with spine-chilling screams?

When his mother the Female Elephant
died of old age Shaka butchered
scores of pregnant women
with his own hands to search
their entrails for the secret of life
and found only blood and gore.
In the dark days that followed
his nation foundered in a bloodbath
until he died like Caesar at the hands
of two brothers and a friend.

Mad Mzilikazi of the Matabele
rivalled Shaka's massacres razing
kraals crops and cattle. Between them
they created a *mfecane* that killed
a million people and left the survivors
in a wasteland of their own making.

What malice in nature permits
such monsters to be born and live?
The savages of Africa are no nobler
than the savages of Europe. Black
is a pigment of the skin, not a moral
or mental condition; it is the business
of dermatologists, not politicians. The art
of massacring the innocent was not invented
on the continent that gave birth to us.
Long before Ashanti warriors subjugated
their neighbours brutally to the Golden Stool
to found a kingdom, the armies of Greece
and Persia, Rome and Babylon, of the Huns
and the Vandals taught the world all there is
to know about pillage rape and slaughter and
at the Cape of Good Hope it was Kitchener
the Lord who invented the concentration camp
Comrade Stalin, Herr Hitler, and Chairman Mao
perfected along with Bosnia's ethnic cleansers.
For every Rwanda there are two Irelands,
for every Bangui three Buchenwalds,
for every Hottentot a score of Huguenots—
from Attila the Hun to Ante Pavelić, the butcher
of Zagreb, from the first city in Mesopotamia
to Mogadishu, from the Crusades to the Khmer Rouge
human history is a grisly calendar of atrocities.

Pink skin too
is a matter
of pigmentation.
Cruelty, thy name
is Man—
civilized Man!
Our most noble
dreams drown
in blood and tears.

I have watched vultures
rip wildebeest to shreds
and hyenas root in entrails
of gazelles with blood-
smeared snout, but they
were feeding on carcasses
not wallowing in the pain
of living kin—like the crack
Canadian paratrooper who
took 4 hours to beat
and kick to death Sidane
a 16-year-old black
in handcuffs in a sand-
bagged cell 7 feet
by 9 feet to teach him
fear while his buddy took
snapshots with a flash
and his superiors listened
to the screams of the dying
boy one night in Somalia.

If I were still as black
as I was born long long ago
I would not want to emulate
a people who live by the cold
knife of logic and remember
only victories, who invented
apartheid to give cruelty
the face of reason. A giraffe
cannot become a monkey,
nor should a monkey want
to be an Arab or an African.
Let's search our own hearts
and histories for the warm
hand of compassion to show us
the true road to freedom where
defeat renders us human
and human is understanding
that we share and share alike
the vulnerable flesh and
the knowledge of our dying
with all men and women
and there must be a way
forward that leads back
to what the birds in the air
and all the beasts on land and
in the sea have never forgotten:
that we are children
of hatching and caring
nestling nursing sharing
and sharing alike.

Even the books are sweating on the shelves
as noon approaches and I wonder if their authors
would approve my celebrating summer in sorrow.

Ideas too are mortal, their half-life measured
not in histories of wealth or war but by the light
they shed in the mind. The tall sunflowers
are gazing bright-eyed across the garden.
Would they if they could approve the war
between the wilderness and civilization
whose beneficiaries they are? The advance
of weeds and seedlings is relentless: wild
raspberry bushes with their clustered flesh,
bristling nettles and blazing-stars, juicy
milkweed with their hooded blooms, goldenrod
and devil's paintbrush, lilac-banded teasel
with their stout spikes, black-eyed Susan,
thistles, mustards, vetches, brambles
and ivies—all pressing whatever advantage
they have gained, using all the strategies
of shading thrusting crowding pushing
jostling to procure their place in the sun.
And we must confront them, keep them at bay,
eradicate them to secure the space we need
for ourselves and all the fruit and vegetables
we have bred too feeble to survive without us
the unforgiving free-for-all of evolution.
Is this the root of evil that we took sides
with the garden against the wilderness,
mastering nature which will be no one's slave?

                    For millions of years
                    our primate ancestors
                    moved with the sun
                    and rains, with the herds
                    and grasses, learning
                    to walk this planet
                    crisscross, carrying

only spear and stone,
fire and the day's
quarry and pickings.
Night was home
by a lake or river
under a mutable
moon and the stars
floating radiant
and mute on the water's
mirror where the first
awed reflection
glimmered then ignited
and flashed in the brain
the whole cosmos
thundered across the face
of the earth the first
question as unanswerable
as the last breath
that made us nomads
of the seasons and the sky.

The fateful breakthrough came some fifty millennia ago.
By that time we were carving boats out of tree trunks
to test the waters and shortly we reached Australia.
We'd eliminated most hominid rivals and soon assimilated
the last of those burly Neanderthals: their big brains
were no match for our brawn. But we learnt a few things
from them about herbal medicine and burying people.
We endured a few more chilling cold spells that lasted
a couple of thousand years and induced us to tailor
our own clothes, but the weather was getting warmer.
Things were improving all around. So we began to craft
bracelets and necklaces, shape pottery figurines,
even paint pictures on the walls of our caves—

we were starting to appreciate beauty, and soon realized
we could do better than mother nature, that heartless bitch.
Art was born. A regular barter trade in ivory, bronze,
and ceramic adornments followed; we shared the profits.
The moon taught us how to divide the cycles of the sun:
calendars are good for religion, keeping appointments
with the gods, and that's good for business because you feast
better when you trade well. Hunting was good too,
plenty of animals, though we may have overdone it a bit:
some of the large ones like giant elk, mammoth,
woolly rhino and diprotodon disappeared—hunted
to extinction they say. But there were more and more
of us, humans were multiplying around the world,
and we *had* to eat. That's when we made the discovery
that changed everything: we learnt to grow and raise
our own food: millet in Africa, maize in America,
rice in Asia, and sheep goats gazelles and oxen
everywhere. No more waiting for mongongo nuts
from fickle nature, no more running after antelopes
till your feet splayed like lily-pads. We made ourselves
independent and settled down to civilization, built
huts temples palaces and filled them with beds benches
tables even vases—and it was all ours: we made it
we owned it and we invented words and numbers
to keep track of things. No more monkey business
for us: for all their chattering and squealing when alarmed
they could barely tell a leopard from a python. No,
we found out what words were good for and we talked
and talked and we're still talking because talking
means progress and progress is what it's all about.

The neolithic revolution overthrew an order
of nature as cataclysmically as any comet.
It began perhaps in the valley of the Nile

whose waters the dark heart of Africa pumps
to the moon's rhythms to flood its banks
and prepare a fertile ground for growing
grain and raising cattle. Nomads settled down
to farming as home ceased to be a harmony
of shifting rains and the resilient ways
of beast and plant, and became a place to stay.
Campsites turned into hamlets, hamlets into
villages into towns and soon Jericho built
walls to protect its harvest from thieves
and *la dolce vita* spread to the valleys
of the Jordan, the Tigris and the Euphrates
till in Anatolia they were weaving cloth
in the first city, Çatal Hüyük, a streetless
hive whose five thousand inhabitants entered
their homes through the roof and buried
the dead under their beds after the birds
had picked them clean—urban civilization
was launched! Herdsmen who sat in the fierce
heat to etch into clay tablets pledges of goats
for the gods unwittingly invented money
and writing. To the north children of a lesser sun
changed colour to permit ultraviolet light
to pass through pink skin to produce
what the long winters deprived them of—
vitamins essential to the strength of bones,
while their parents tamed the first horses
whose descendants would carry apocalyptic hordes
from one end of the world to the other.
The harvest they reaped we call history.

                    The seeds of war and malice were born
                        when we began to work the earth
                          for comforts and pleasures only

power and wealth could buy.
The larger your house the larger
your appetite for things to put in it
until you become so ravenous to own
that you will kill to slake your appetite
for property
but by then you have built
a still larger house
creating a still larger appetite.

Everything was implicit in the beginning
which was no beginning if the universe
is a closed system where probability
puts things in their places though you
can't be sure where anything ever is
except on its way down for energy
is constant and nothing is lost
except form by the second law
of thermodynamics life is motion
is heat is irreversible even when
the temperature was ten quadrillion
degrees and light had only travelled
three centimetres from nowhere a hundred
picoseconds after nothing ceased to exist
permanence had vanished from a vacuum
to make room for entropy moving quarks
to particles it was all settled a millisecond
after reality became probable transience formed
plasma atoms molecules elements life a whole
universe composed of 18 quarks, and every creature
wanting immortality makes dying copies of itself
so that its kind will last forever—so shall we
go on pursuing power when we know the copies
aren't exact and the mistakes in time

will turn our kind into another, leaving
only a sketchy record of the dead ends
in the DNA? Shall we go on killing one another
when we know something is lost in every change
in every transformation energy always runs down
volts itself into other orders below the horizon
of recovery so that the universe is cooling off
and fifty sun years from now our star
will grow hot and bloated with exhaustion
and explode all myths of eternity spinning
a ball of ash beyond any orbit of life—
how can we not share the planet we share
when we know we must share its fate?

They shared out Africa amongst fifteen European nations
wheeling and dealing in Berlin in 1884, like frenzied vultures
they tore a living continent to shreds, hacking and pecking
for the lion's share. High as euphoria they sent their soldiers
to draw a map of Africa in their own superior image—
the arrogant English, the intolerant French, the brutal
Portuguese, the imperious Germans and the rest of them,
obsessed with overseas possessions they sliced and slashed
across 850 languages to stake out their claims in Akan
Bobangi Chewa Dagomba Edo Fulani Gandi Herero Kikuyu
Kiswahili Luo Xhosa Yao Zulu to cut across the lands
the territories of a thousand tribes and clans, Bushmen
and Bantu, Hamites, Kaffirs and Pygmies—and the
missionaries came with their pious anaesthetics the better
to rob Africa of its gods its legends its dances its gold,
and teach the natives the gospel of forgiveness and of scorning
worldly goods so that the merchants could come smug
with their air of euphoria to relieve them of those goods
that were so bad for their souls, turning the richest
continent on earth into a poorhouse within a single century.

It's always you and I, black
or white, who must pay
for the privileges of the pious
and the powerful. The Che
Guevaras and Bikos who would
set us free become their victims.
This is the month Jaurès, the people's
warrior for peace, was murdered
in Paris and the echo of the shots
a feeble-minded Serb student fired
reverberated in the corridors
of profit and politics, sending
Europe's statesmen into a shuttle
frenzy to replace *la realité du monde
sensible* with the illusions of war
and victory in which Africa was
but a pawn and for some a prize.

The ides of July have come
and the rainy season approaches.
Africa is calling *uhuru* across
its deserts, mountains and lakes
and the echo wakes the spirits
of the ancestors to dance with them
from the darkness of fear and superstition
into the light of freedom: *uhuru*
is the voice of its forests, rivers
and savannahs where a pageant of furs
and feathers, hoofs and horns,
stripes and spots celebrates
the improbable odds of survival.
Across the Serengeti plain
north through the Maasai Mara
proud nomads still herd

their cattle with the seasons
where a lion pride rests and plays
under the umbrella of an acacia tree
side by side with a sly hyena
and a cheeky family of baboons
zebras graze amongst skittish
gazelles and wildebeest to hide
their giveaway camouflage; red-faced
the ground hornbill walk among them
muttering through their crimson wattles
while on a kopje where a lethal
puffadder sleeps a topi stands
tall as if to impale the sky
with its ridged horns, watching
the swift and abrupt impala
leap high and wide of nothing
anyone can see while above them
an eagle's cry draws ominous
circles no larger than a kraal
that narrows like a closing net.
In the big bush to the west
black mambas drape like lianas
over jungle branches and siafu
killer ants advance in deadly
formations that stop short of
nothing. Ants have crawled
and snakes slid and tongued
their devious ways voiceless
through a paradise of thickets
for two hundred million years
while apes and monkeys are barely
in their salad days, the bright-eyed
chimps agile in the canopy
and the gorillas lumbering already
into the last remote range

of their lives. By the watering-hole
at the edge of night the leopard's
throaty call troubles the thirst
of those who come to drink.
Darkness too feeds on freedom.
When Africa calls *uhuru* the echo
reverberates around the earth
for it speaks with the voice
of the birds in the air and all
the beasts on land and in the water
who have always known that life
is a celebration of just being there.

This is the month
Kafka was born and
Jean-Jacques died.
Grimpez aux arbres,
espèces de singes!
Retour à la nature!
Journey from grey
penthouse back to
green canopy by
memories that were
even then infested
with snakes. Proust
was born this month
to search and find
his jungle Eden in
a cork-lined room
where he smelled
his way back
to many beginnings.
Something was lost
on the way to the city

for Joseph K. to wake
and discover freedom
was his prison
or else why
would any human
turn into a beetle?

Houses are the atoms that constitute cities
temples and palaces the atoms of power
combine easily to form the molecules of hatred
and war unless you block the reactions
of greed and fear that catalyze them. Houses cry
for windows and windows cry for air and light.
Beware of those in pursuit of power, whatever
colour their skin, however pious their mask,
lest they put shutters and bars on your windows
and lock your doors, for power needs victims
and henchmen to violate you throw you
scraps so you'll violate others to get more
scraps for power is voracious as vultures
and money is power's club, it will put you
in your place buy your women, your sons
your daughters, and sooner or later your mind
and your heart, turning temples and palaces
into prisons till it possesses everything,
consumes everything till all that is left
is to consume itself
leaving a wasteland

like Rwanda
where in a single month
half a million children
women and men were clubbed
hacked stabbed chopped

kicked and gouged to death
by their good friends and
neighbours disembowelled
decapitated and left to rot
in their kitchens and bedrooms
in the fields and by the roadsides
till a stench more putrid than
the one-day bloom of a thousand
stinking euphorbia flowers
drove the people from their homes
their families their villages
to escape genocide the Tutsis
and the Hutus like the Ibo
slaughtered till the rivers
ran black with blood shed
by black clubs and machete
the survivors fleeing between
Jalaf and Khalif, too famished
to run for their lives
through Angola and Mozambique,
Somalia and the Sudan,
Namibia and Zaire, men
dragging their indignities
through the dust, women
balancing their poverty
on their heads, and harried
children, with names as
auspicious as Lakayana
and Mamadow, but with eyes
like Rosita's full of the pain
and horror they cannot comprehend
the homeless driven by hunger
and terror all across Africa
to camps where millions more
will die from cholera, diarrhea
and numb hopelessness

till the poet runs out of words:
Mother, mother—why
why was I born
black? Why
was I born?

Harambee, my beloved
Africa, *harambee*!
You need not be a continent of refugees.
Five hundred years of slavery
will end when you end them.
They left the chains, but you can make
kitchen utensils of them or
cast them in the sea and take back
your pride. You need not kiss
or grease the hands of any master.
And the fifty flags you inherited
belie your true nature. Banish
the monsters of Mogadishu and
Kigali, Addis Ababa and Bangui,
Moroni, Usumbura and Katanga,
whose fortunes the *mzungu*
propped up without shame.
Slavery is now an affliction
of the mind, and when *uhuru*
echoes through its convoluted
corridors loud enough to command
us all to embrace each other
Africa will be free at last.

Dance, my beloved
Africa, dance
for you are free

to choose freedom now.
You cannot live
on *ugali* or *foufou* alone.
The joy of life feeds
on *uhuru*, and *uhuru*
feeds on knowing
that you are flying
at a few hundred km/sec
through an exploding universe
that cares for us only
when we care for each other
and that like the space
around us we fly apart
unless love holds us together.
Don't let any *toubab* say
that bringing harmony
to Africa is like trying
to play a violin
by pissing on it.
Let us join hands
in a hundred dances
an ancient courage
has choreographed
to confront our enemies
inside and outside
the kraal of our skin.

Sing, my beloved Africa,
for the riches of the earth
are still within you—
gold and diamonds, uranium
phosphates platinum oil
and iron, waiting
by a million acres
of untilled soil

for you to share
amongst your people.
Sing not of pulas
or dalásis, kwachars
shillings or zaires—
sing of the heart's treasures
and the mind's triumphs,
sing of Biko and Hani
and the nameless heroes
of your many histories,
sing of your rivers and savannahs
of *babae watoto*, the owl's curse,
and the blessing of sacred trees
and mountains, for Africa calls:
uhuru uhuru uhuru!

The sun has reached its zenith now and the trees
are standing in a pool of their own shade.
The light is so green against a golden sky
I might be living in a hot summer's dream
where lovers float silent as photosynthesis
on the green leaves of their affections,
embracing the knowledge that they go to seed
a new generation, mixing chromosomes with passion
on the off-chance they might surprise the future
and go beyond the stars. Haunted by hummingbirds
viper's bugloss bristles its deep blue forget-me-not
by the pond while in the garden blister beetles
bleed to ward off predators. Like the tawny lily
that blooms for one day only though its green sword
is drawn for the whole season, you and I are
day flowers lost in the wasteland of eternity
with only a song to ward off the night.

Acknowledgements

When Africa Calls Uhuru was first published as section 5 of an epic work-in-progress which I called *Seasons of Blood*, it started with "… the last cry / of six-year-old Rosita / beheaded with a machete / after they hacked off her feet / in …" El Salvador which signified the violent colonialism of America in Spanish-speaking South and Central America. *Seasons of Blood* quickly became a search for the origin and history of our brutal humanity in different parts of the world. The first six sections were published by BuschekBooks in Ottawa in 2011.The seventh section, *Footprints of Dark Energy,* in a collection of poems with the same title, was published by Guernica Editions and it won the Ottawa Book Award in 2020.

I acknowledge my gratitude to the Kenyan writer Francis Imbuga who generously introduced me to his home country when I went to Kenya to do research for *When Africa Calls* Uhuru.

Guernica Editions is now publishing my seventh book of poetry over just a few years and it has been a satisfying and enlightening experience. I am grateful for the intelligent and serious attention that has been paid to my work and I appreciate the aesthetic presentation of the books.

Finally, I want to thank my wife, Arlette Francière, for her tireless and inspired proofreading of the poem.

About the Author

Henry Beissel is a poet, playwright, fiction writer, translator and editor with 45 books published. Among the 25 collections of poetry are his epic *Seasons of Blood* and the lyrical *Stones to Harvest* as well as his celebration of Canada in *Cantos North*, the 364 haiku in *What if Zen Gardens ...*, a finalist for the Ottawa Book Awards, and the visionary *Footprints of Dark Energy*, which won First Prize in the Ottawa Book Awards in 2020. As a playwright, Henry came to international fame with *Inuk and the Sun* which premièred at the Stratford Festival in 1973 and has since been translated into many languages and performed internationally. He is Distinguished Emeritus Professor at Concordia University (Montreal) where he taught English Literature for 30 years and founded a Creative Writing program that is still flourishing today. Henry lives in Ottawa with his wife Arlette Francière, the literary translator and artist.

Henry Beissel Poetry Collections

WITNESS THE HEART   Toronto: Willow Green Press, 1963

NEW WINGS FOR ICARUS   Toronto: Coach House Press, 1966 (with lithographs by Norman Yates)

THE WORLD IS A RAINBOW   Toronto: Canadian Music Centre, 1968. (A collection of poems for children set to music by Wolfgang Bottenberg)

FACE ON THE DARK   Toronto: New Press, 1970

THE SALT I TASTE   Montreal: DC Books, 1975

CANTOS NORTH   Alexandria: Ayorama Editions, 1980 (Deluxe edition with lithographs by Friedhelm Lach). Moonbeam: Penumbra Press, 1982

SEASON OF BLOOD   Toronto: Mosaic Press, 1984

POEMS NEW AND SELECTED   Toronto: Mosaic Press, 1987

AMMONITE   Alexandria: Ayorama Editions, 1987 (Deluxe edition with artwork by Friedhelm Lach)

STONES TO HARVEST   Alexandria: Ayorama Editions, 1987 (Deluxe edition with woodcuts by Dale Alpen-Whiteside) Goderich: Moonstone Press, 1993

DYING I WAS BORN   Waterloo: Penumbra Press, 1992 (with woodcuts by Peter Schwarz)

"Where Shall the Birds Fly?" (No. 4 in the SEASONS OF BLOOD cycle) in RAGING LIKE A FIRE   Montreal: Vehicule Press, 1993 and in INTER-PLAYS WORKS AND WORDS OF WRITERS AND CRITICS   St. John's (NF), 1994

THE DRAGON & THE PEARL   Ottawa: BuschekBooks, 2002

ACROSS THE SUN'S WARP   Ottawa: BuschekBooks, 2003

A METEOROLOGY OF LOVE   Thornhill: Beret Days Press, 2010

COMING TO TERMS WITH A CHILD   Windsor: Black Moss Press, 2011

SEASONS OF BLOOD Ottawa: BuschekBooks, 2011

FUGITIVE HORIZONS   Toronto: Guernica Editions, 2013

COMING TO TERMS WITH A CHILD / EIN KIND KOMMT ZUR SPRACHE
   Marburg (Germany): Verlag LiteraturWissenschaft, 2015
FUGITIVE HORIZONS / FLÜCHTIGE HORIZONTE   Translator: Heide
   Fruth-Sachs   Marburg (Germany): Verlag LiteraturWissenschaft, 2015
SIGHTLINES   Toronto: Guernica Editions, 2016
CANTOS NORTH/CANTOS DU NORD   Traduction : Arlette Francière
   Toronto: Guernica Editions, 2017
WHAT IF ZEN GARDENS ...   Toronto: Guernica Editions, 2017
FOOTPRINTS OF DARK ENERGY   Toronto: Guernica Editions, 2019
STONES TO HARVEST/ESCARMOUCHES DE LA CHAIR Traduction:
   Arlette Francière Toronto: Guernica Editions, 2022
WHEN AFRICA CALLS *UHURU*   Hamilton: Guernica Editions, 2023

Poetry Translations

THE PRICE OF MORNING   Vancouver: Prism International Press, 1968
   (translation of poems by Walter Bauer)
A DIFFERENT SUN   Ottawa: Oberon Press, 1976 (translation of poems
   by Walter Bauer)
A THISTLE IN HIS MOUTH   Dunvegan: Cormorant Books, 1987 (trans-
   lation of poems by Peter Huchel)
LETTERS ON BIRCHBARK   Ottawa: Penumbra Press, 2000 (translation
   of poems by Uta Regoli)

Printed in February 2023
by Gauvin Press,
Gatineau, Québec